I0841181

Vol 6

MAZE

Ages 4-6

FOR KIDS

MAZE BOOK

SOCIAL MEDIA

/MySweetBooks1

/MySweetBooks1

/MySweetBooks1

/MySweetBooks

Email Us : mysweetbooks1@gmail.com

Printed in USA
Published by My Sweet Books

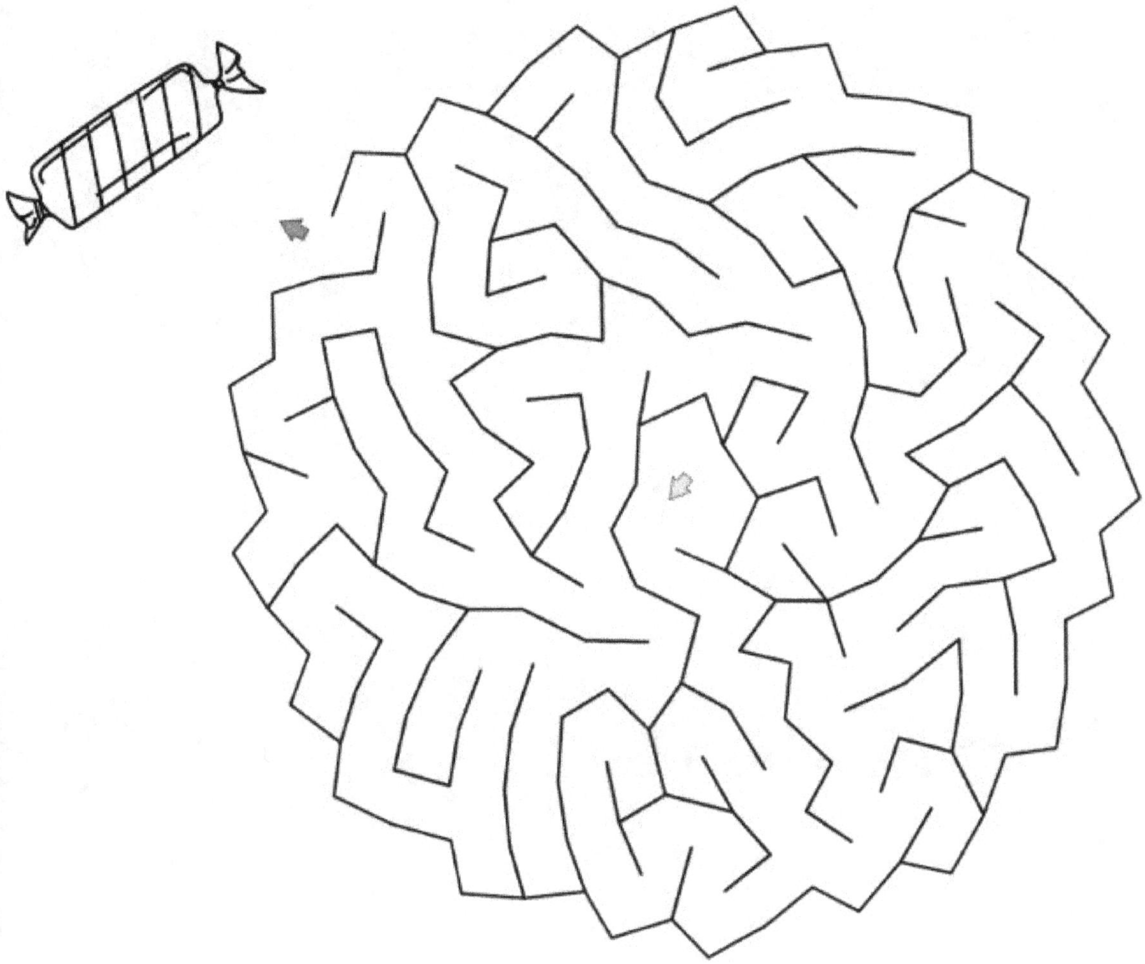

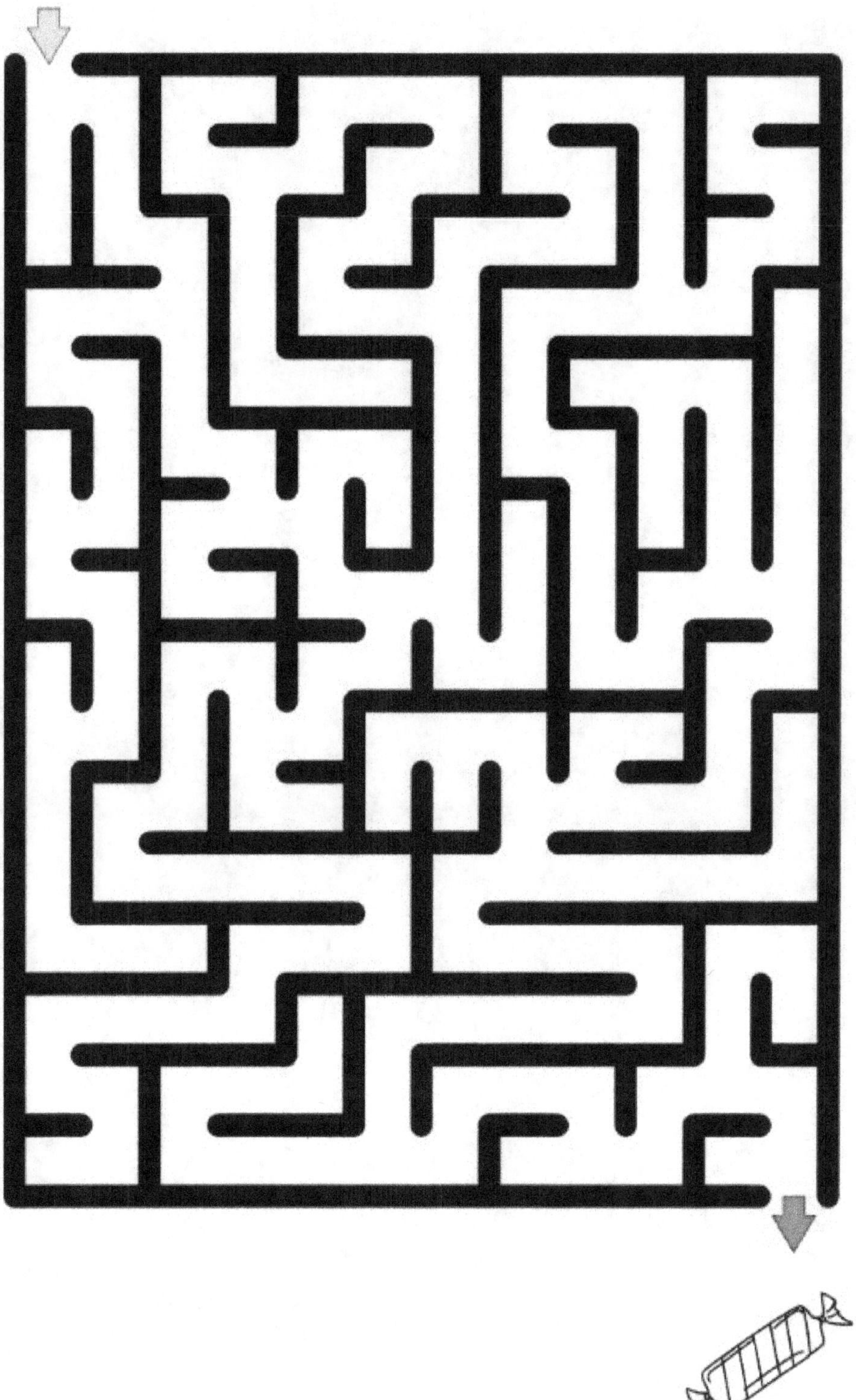

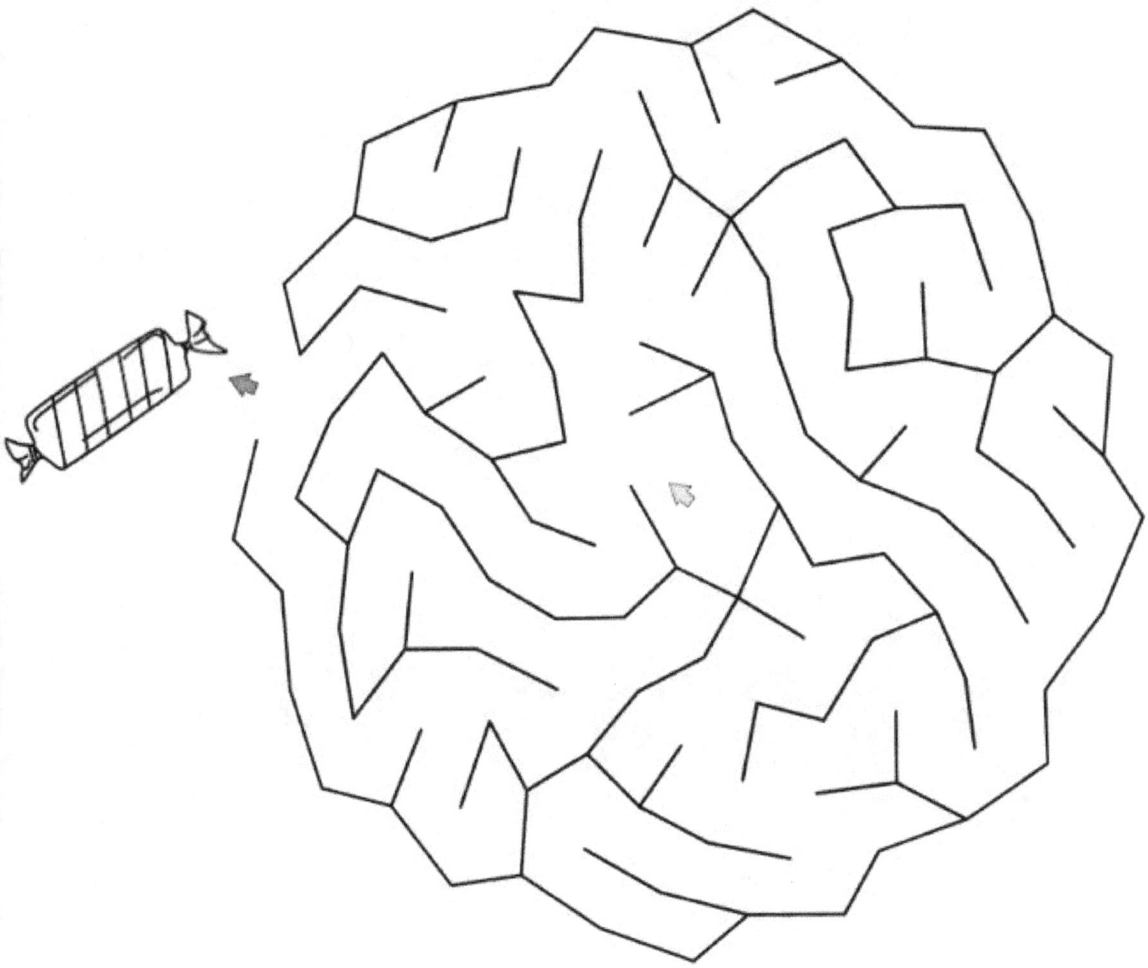

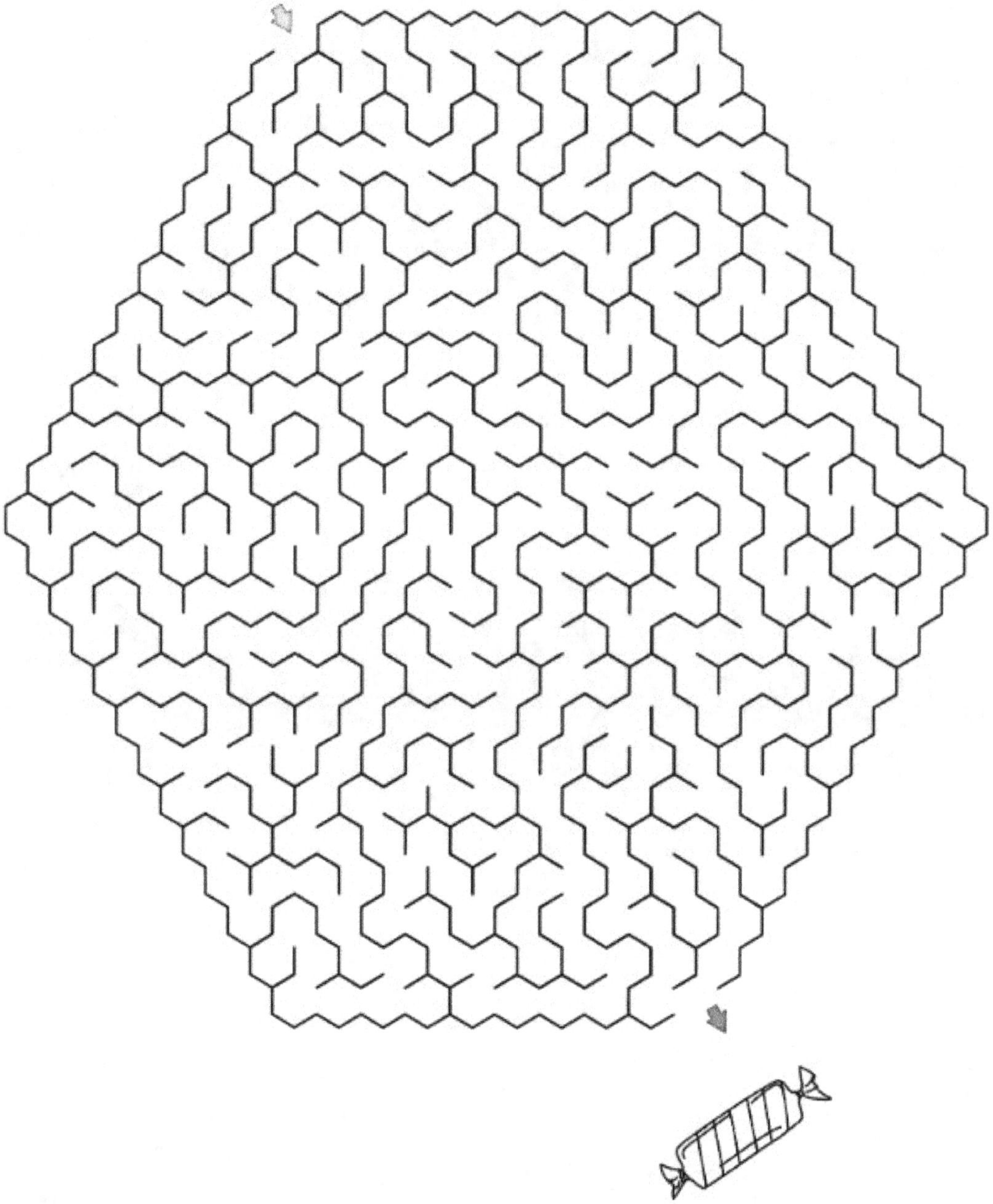

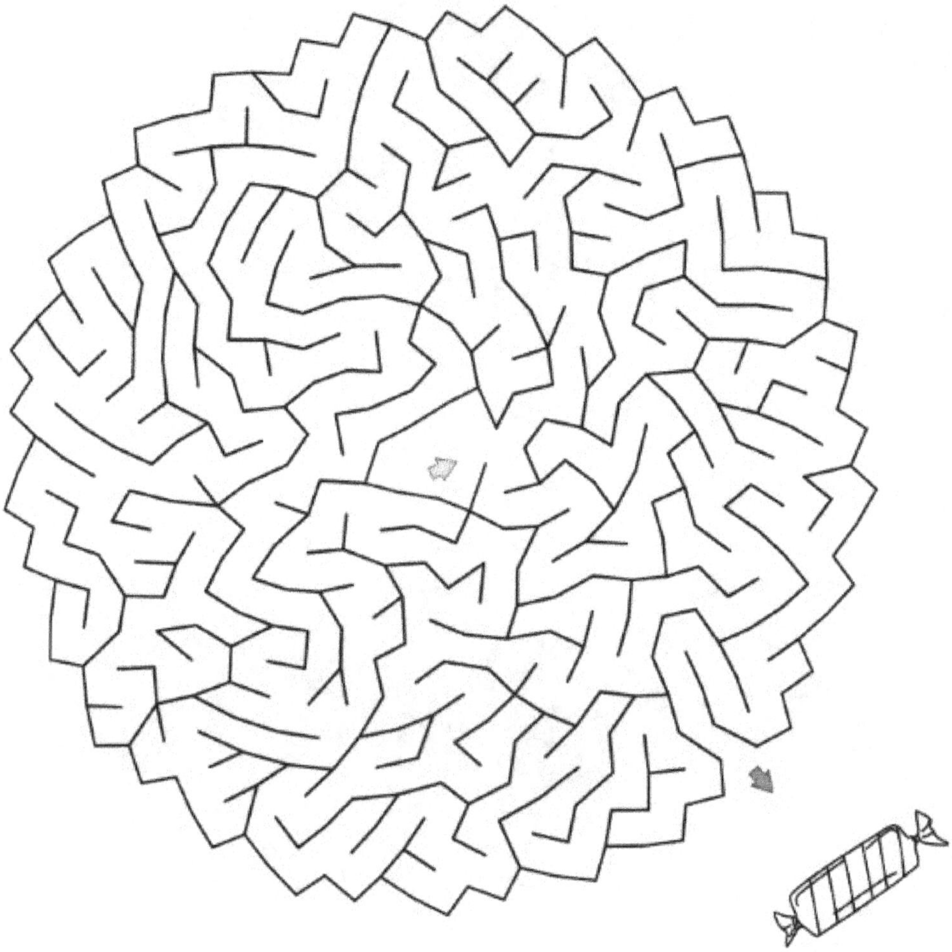

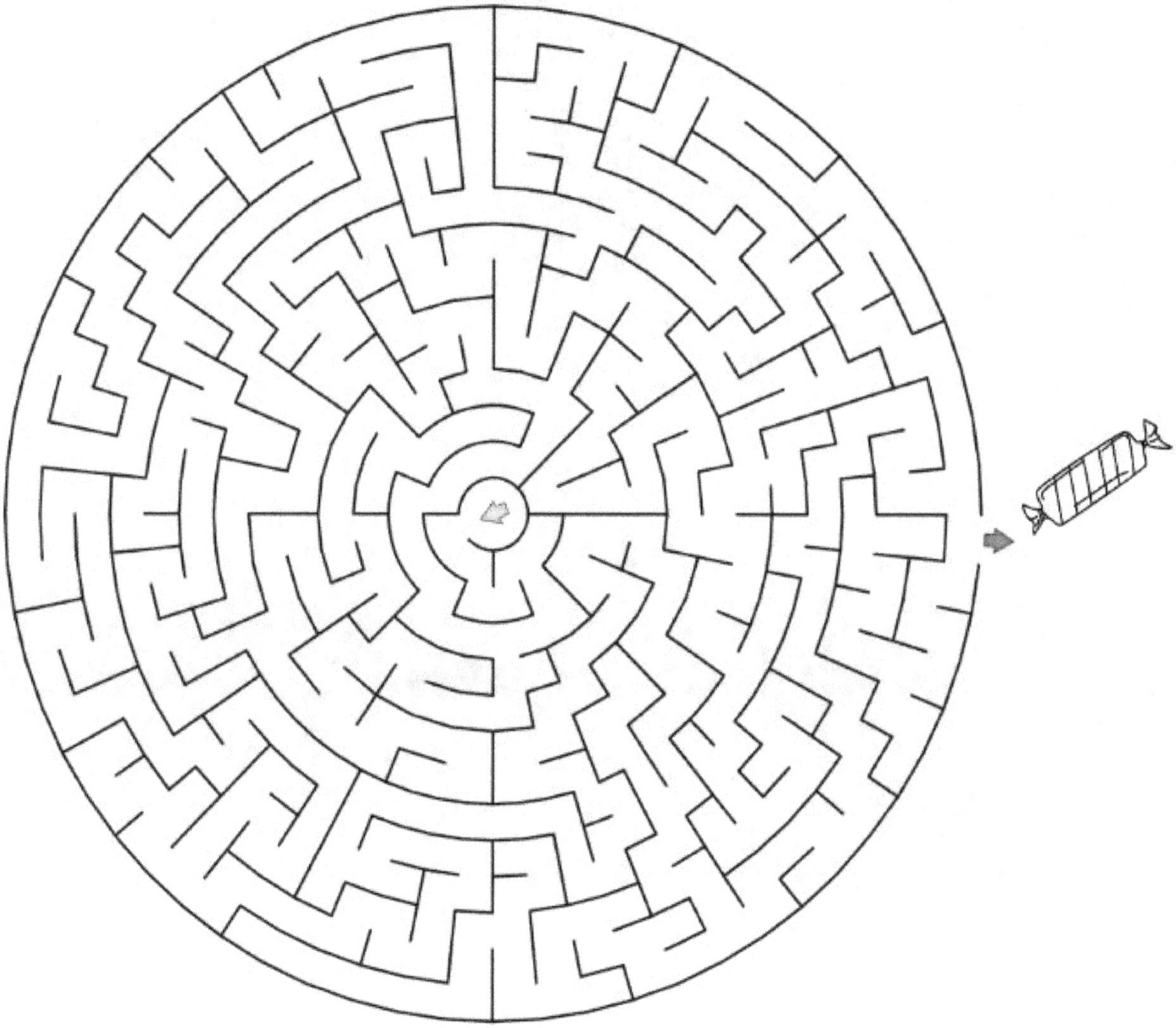

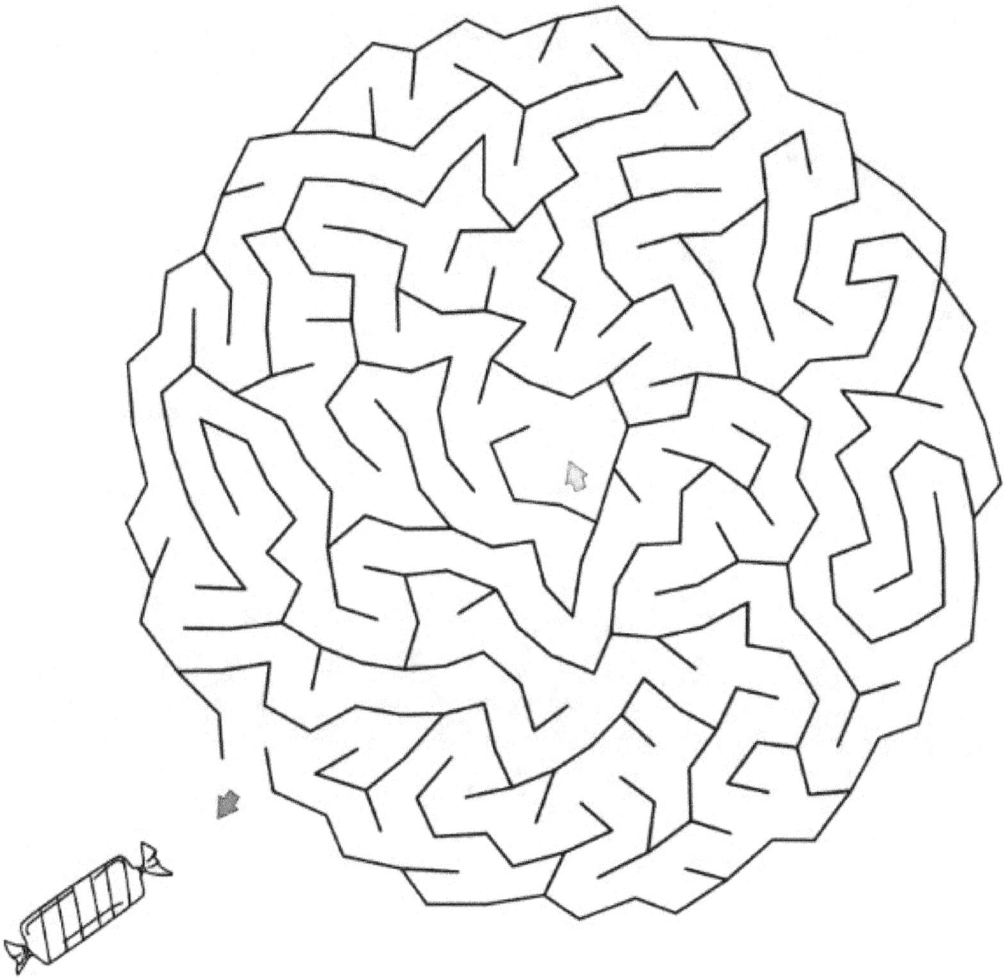

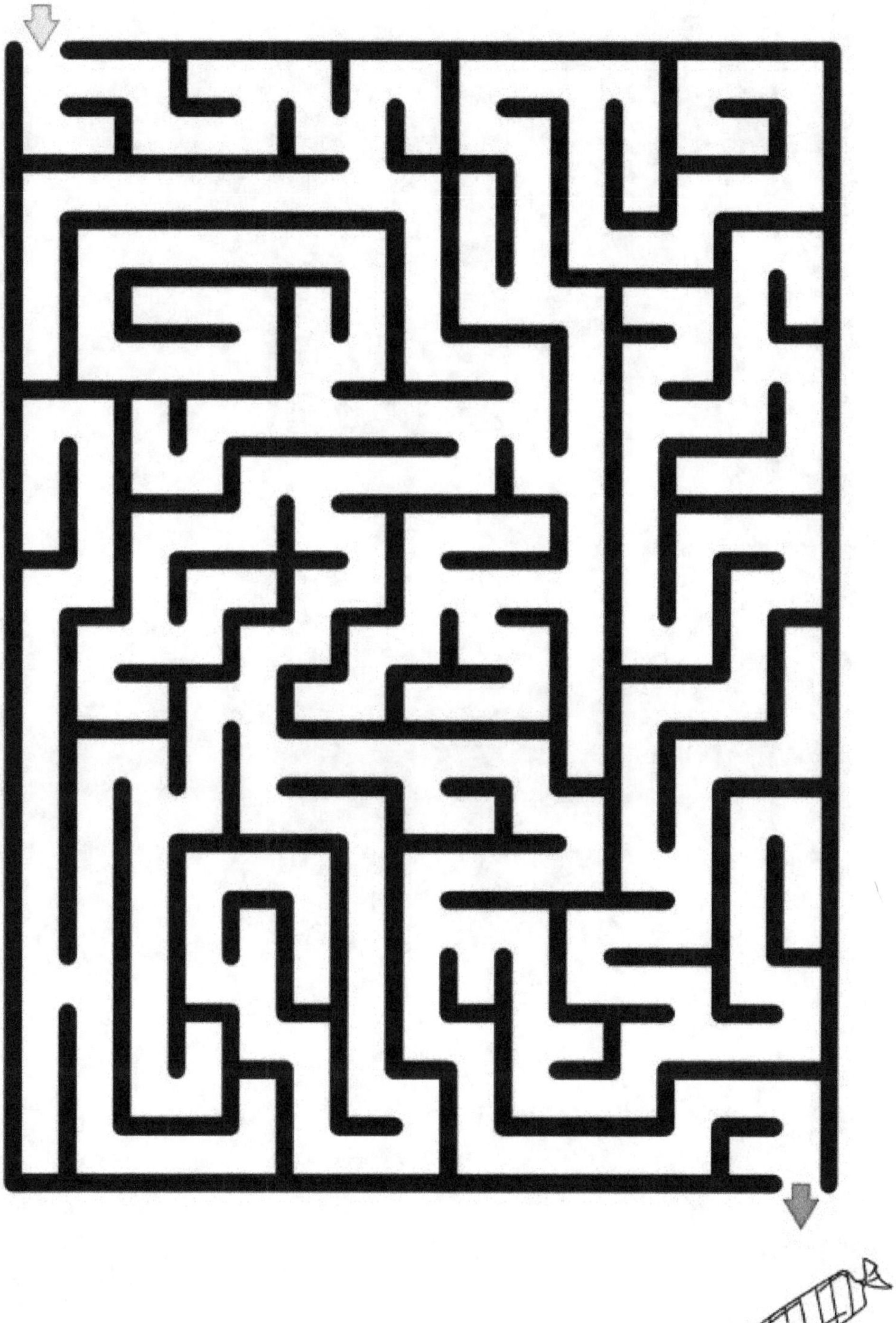

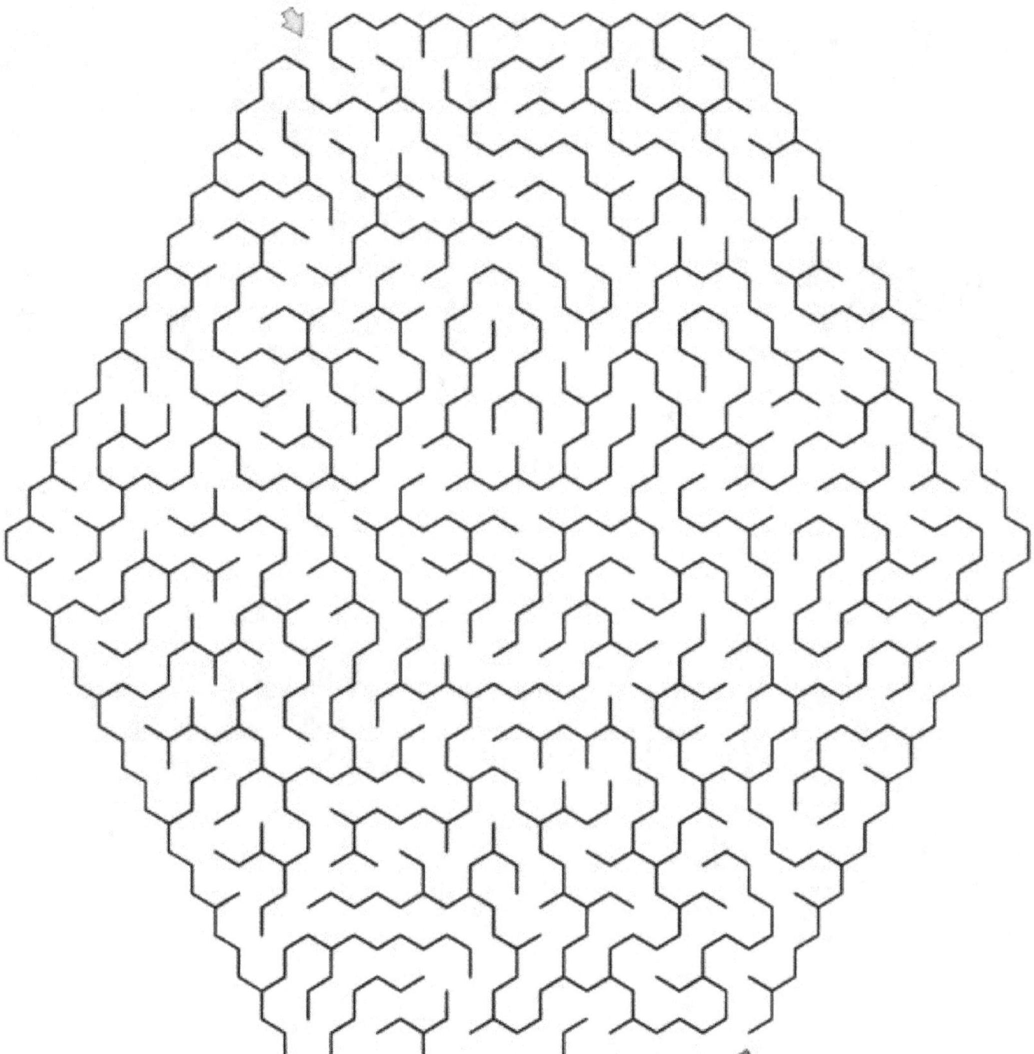

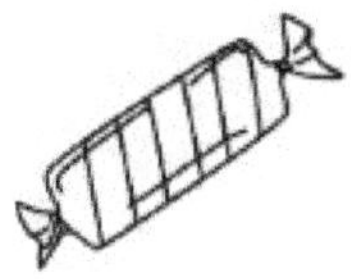

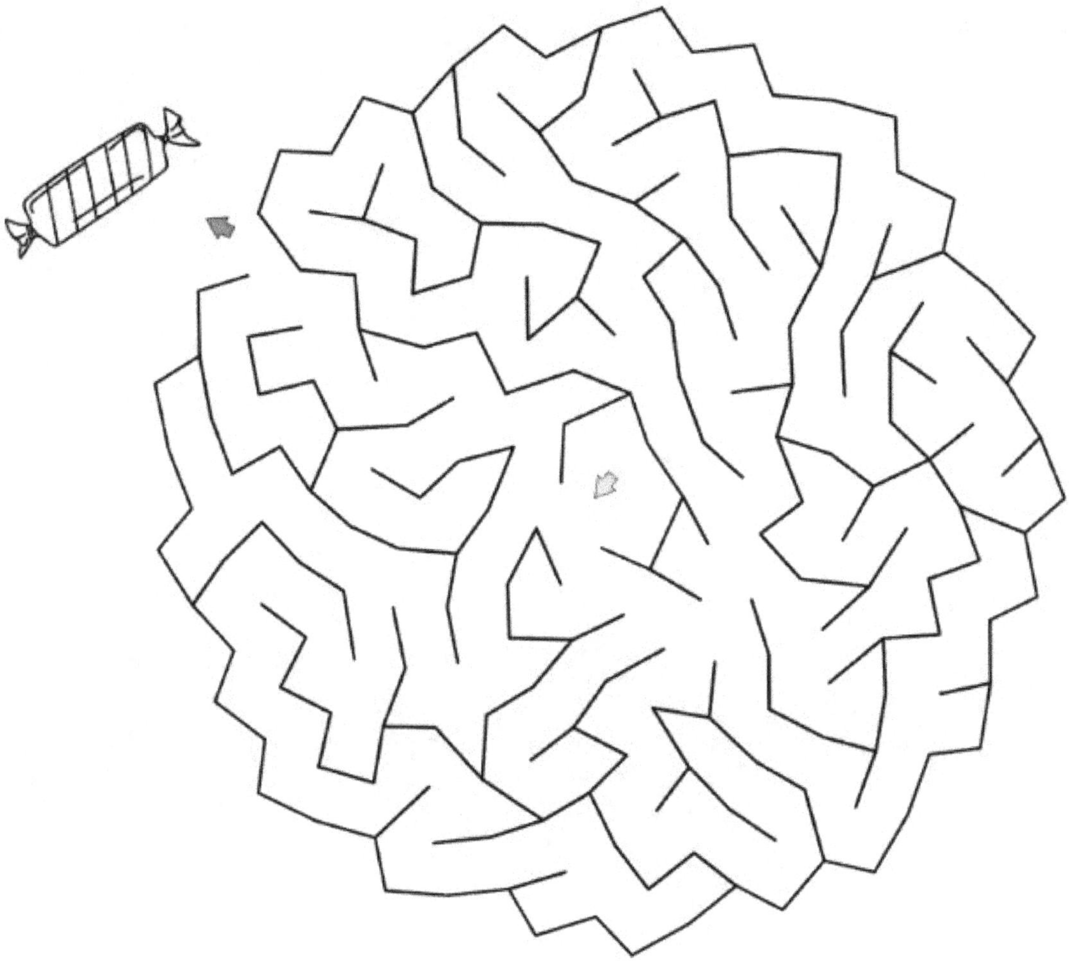

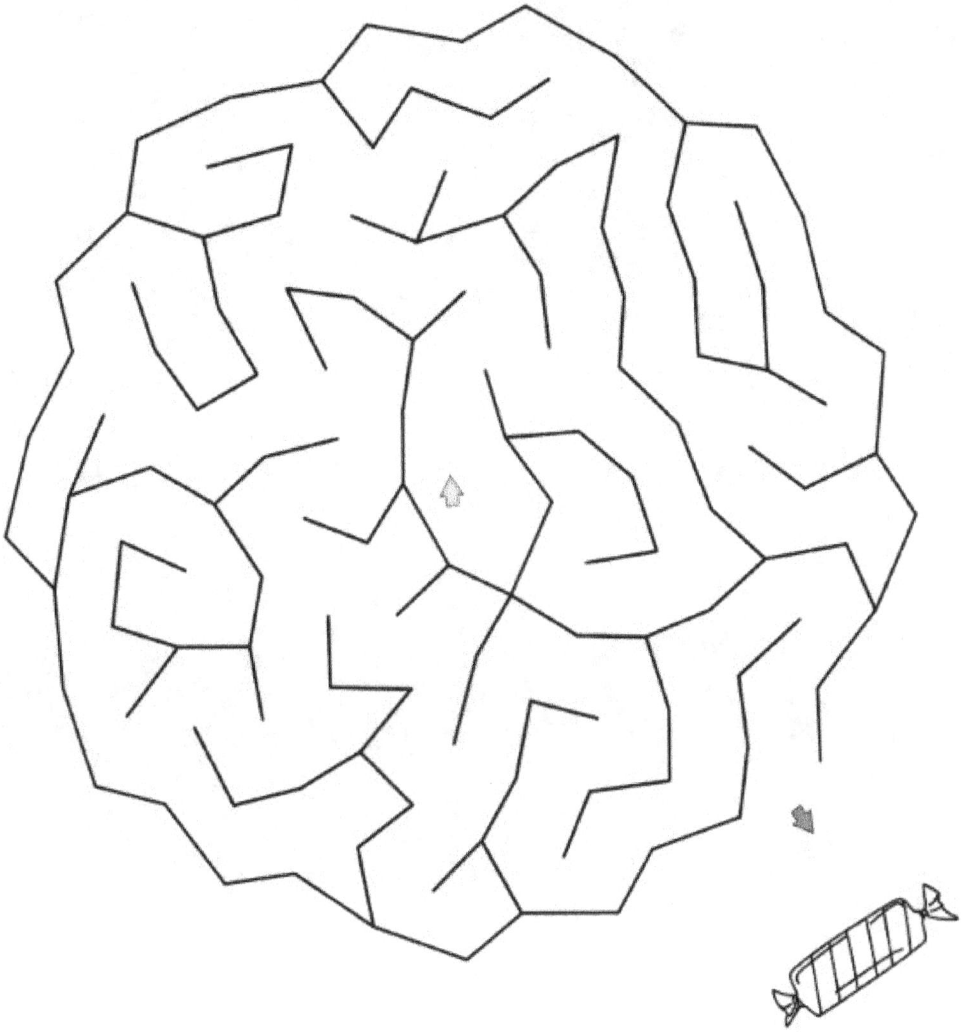

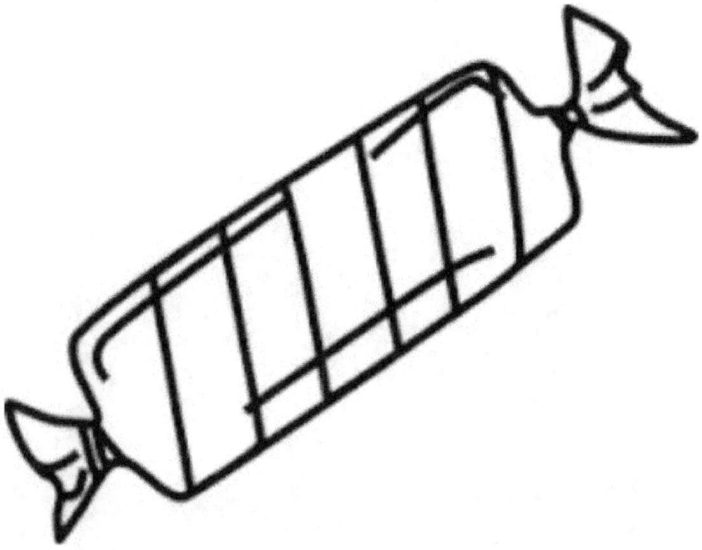

www.ingramcontent.com/pod-product-compliance
Lightning Source LLC
Chambersburg PA
CBHW081736250726
48657CB00010B/3296
9781704657585